QAno

QAnon and the Impact on Our Social Life, Covid-19 and 5G Theories Explained

Blake Harris

© Copyright 2021 by

All rights reserved.

This document is geared towards providing exact and reliable information with regards to the topic and issue covered. The publication is sold with the idea that the publisher is not required to render accounting, officially permitted, or otherwise, qualified services. If advice is necessary, legal or professional, a practiced individual in the profession should be ordered.

From a Declaration of Principles which was accepted and approved equally by a Committee of the American Bar Association and a Committee of Publishers and Associations.

In no way is it legal to reproduce, duplicate, or transmit any part of this document in either electronic means or in printed format. Recording of this publication is strictly prohibited and any storage of this document is not allowed unless with written permission from the publisher. All rights reserved.

The information provided herein is stated to be truthful and consistent, in that any liability, in terms of inattention or otherwise, by any usage or abuse of any policies, processes, or directions contained within is the solitary and utter responsibility of the recipient reader. Under no circumstances will any legal responsibility or blame be held against the publisher for any reparation, damages, or monetary loss due to the information herein, either directly or indirectly.

Respective authors own all copyrights not held by the publisher.

The information herein is offered for informational purposes solely, and is universal as so. The presentation of the information is without contract or any type of guarantee assurance.

The trademarks that are used are without any consent, and the publication of the trademark is without permission or backing by the trademark owner. All trademarks and brands within this book are for clarifying purposes only and are the owned by the owners themselves, not affiliated with this document.

TABLE OF CONTENTS

INTRODUCTION 6
Chapter 1: THE GENESIS OF QAnon 10
Chapter 2: THE INTERVIEW 26
    WHO ARE Q? 36
    REASON VERSUS FAITH 42
    THE APOCALYPSE 46
Chapter 3: THE BOOM IN THE CORONAVIRUS CONSPIRACY 49
Chapter 4: TECHNOLOGY AND COVID 19 59
    A POLLUTED ATMOSPHERE 59
    THE ORIGIN STORY 63
    THE 5 G CONSPIRACY 69
    DEBUNKING THE 5G CONSPIRACY 71
    THE Bill GATES' CONSPIRACY THEORY 75
Chapter 5: SOCIAL MANIPULATION 83
Chapter 6: THE ALLEGATIONS AGAINST QAnon 90
CONCLUSION 97

INTRODUCTION

Conspiracy theories are a staple in American history, and they are tempting to be dismissed as contradictory. However, as the 21st century has progressed, such dismissal has started requiring deliberate blindness. In 2011, when Donald Trump laid the groundwork for a presidential run by openly challenging whether Barack Obama was born in Hawaii, I was a city hall reporter for a local investigative-news site called Honolulu Civil Beat, as all the evidence and records indicate. Trump maintained that Obama was originally born in Africa and was thus not a native American — making him ineligible for the highest office. In our Honolulu newsroom, I recall the debate: Should we even report this "birther" madness?

Nine years later, when news of a terrifying new virus unexpectedly appeared, and with Trump now president, a series of ideas began to burst in the QAnon community: that the coronavirus could not be real; that if it had been, it would have been generated by the "Deep State," the star chamber of government officials and other powerful figures secretly running the world; that the hysteria surrounding the pandemic was part of it. Any of these proposals will make room for Fox News and the public comments of the President. According to The New York Times, at least 145 times, Trump had retweeted accounts that had mostly centered on conspiracy theories, like those of QAnon.

Early on, the power of the internet was known. Still, the very essence of that power — it's the capacity to break every sense of common truth, destroy the framework of civil society and democratic governance — was not. The internet also allowed unknown people to reach millions of people, which Marshall McLuhan never dreamed of at a scale. The warping of common truth causes a man to attack a pizza shop with an AR-15 rifle. It creates online forums where people colorfully imagine a former secretary of state is assassinated. It offers the promise of a Great Awakening, which will route the insiders and expose the truth. It causes chat sites to come alive with commentary speculating that the pandemic of coronavirus could be the moment QAnon waited for. None like that could have been conceived as late as the turn of the century.

QAnon is emblematic of, and their passion for, the sensitivity of modern America to conspiracy theories focused to researching the truth.

Chapter 1: THE GENESIS OF QAnon

The roots of QAnon are recent, but even so, it can be difficult to distinguish myth from fact. One place to start is with Edgar Maddison Welch, a profoundly religious father of two, who had lived an unusual life in the small town of Salisbury, North Carolina, until Sunday, December 4, 2016. Welch gathered his cellphone that morning, a box of shotgun shells, and three loaded guns — a 9-mm AR-15 rifle, a Colt caliber six-shot revolver, and a shotgun — and jumped into his Toyota Prius. He drove 360 miles to a well-to-do neighborhood in Northwest Washington, D.C., parked his car, placed the revolver at his waist in a holster; kept the AR-15 gun around his chest; and walked through the front door of a pizzeria called Comet Ping Pong.

Comet happens to be the spot where my then-baby daughter took her first-ever drink of water on a Sunday afternoon two years ago. There, children gather after soccer games on Saturdays with their parents and teammates, and local bands play on the weekends. In the back, kids challenge their grandparents to Ping-Pong matches as they wait for their pizzas to come out of the restaurant's big clay oven. Comet Ping Pong is a popular Washington venue.

People found Welch straight away that day. In most social settings, an AR-15 rifle makes for a conspicuous sash, but particularly in a position like Comet. As parents, children, and employees hurried outside, several still chewing, Welch started to move through the restaurant, at one point trying to use a butter knife to pry open a locked door, before giving up and firing several rounds from his rifle into the window. There was a tiny computer-storage closet just behind the entrance. That was not what he had planned.

Welch had moved to Washington because of a conspiracy theory, now famously known as Pizzagate, which alleged that Hillary Clinton ran out of Comet Ping Pong with a child sex ring. The idea emerged in October 2016, when WikiLeaks published a cache of emails stolen from John Podesta's account, a former White House staff chief, and then Clinton's presidential campaign chair; Comet was repeatedly listed in exchanges with restaurant owner James Alefantis and others. The emails were primarily about fundraising activities, but high-profile pro – Donald Trump figures, including Mike Cernovich and Alex Jones, began pushing the argument that the emails were evidence of ritualistic child abuse — which emerged in trollish internet corners (such as 4chan) and then spread to more open precincts (Twitter, YouTube). Some conspiracy theorists have said it took place in Comet's basement, where there is no basement. The references to "pizza" and "pasta" in the emails have been interpreted as code words for "children" and "young boys."

Shortly after Trump's victory, as Pizzagate was booming through the internet, Welch began watching conspiracy theory videos on YouTube. He tried to enlist support from at least two people to carry out a guerrilla attack, texting them about his willingness to risk "the lives of a few for the lives of many" and battling "a crooked machine that kidnaps, tortures, and rapes babies and children in our backyard."

Welch seems to have earnestly assumed that at Comet Ping Pong, children were being treated. His family and friends wrote on his behalf letters to the judge describing him as a loving father, a devout Christian, and a man who has gone out of his way to care about others. Welch had specialized in firefighting as a volunteer. He'd gone with the local Baptist Men's Association on an earthquake-response trip to Haiti. A friend from his church said, "He shows the actions of a person who seeks to understand and apply biblical truth." Welch himself expressed what seemed to be sincere remorse, writing in a handwritten note sent by his lawyers to the judge: "It was never my intention to injure or frighten innocent lives, but I now realize how foolish and careless my decision was."

Pizzagate was quickly disappearing. Some of its most prominent supporters, including Jack Posobiec, a conspiracy theorist who is now a reporter for One America News Network, the pro-Trump cable-news channel, have backed up. Alex Jones, who runs the conspiracy-theory website Infowars and hosts a related radio show, apologizes for supporting Pizzagate in the face of the specter of legal action by Alefantis.

Although Welch may have expressed remorse, he did not give any indication that he had stopped believing in the underlying message of Pizzagate: that a group of influential leaders raped children and got away with it. Judging from a burst of internet activity, several people had found ways to step past the episode of Comet Ping Pong and stay focused on what they saw as the greater reality. If you've been paying attention to the right voices on the right pages, you might see in real-time how Pizzagate's central concepts were replicated, updated, and reinterpreted. The millions of people paying attention to sites like 4chan and Reddit will continue to learn about this clandestine and untouchable cabal, about its malignant acts and intentions, about its connections to the left-wing and particularly to the Democrats and Clinton; about its bloodlust and moral degeneration. You might also read about a tiny but swelling band of underground American patriots fighting back-and this would prove important.

Taken together, all this established a philosophy that would soon have a name: QAnon, derived from a mysterious man, "Q," posting on 4chan anonymously. QAnon does not have a physical venue, but it does have an infrastructure, literature, an increasing community of adherents, and much merchandising. It also exhibits other key attributes lacking by Pizzagate. It has the complexity and adaptability to maintain a campaign of this nature over time in the face of inconvenient evidence. For QAnon, any inconsistency can be explained away; no sort of argument against it can prevail.

And we are probably closer than the end to the start of its narrative. The community harnesses fear of a deep sense of belonging and fervent hope. How it breathes life into an ancient end-time problem is profoundly new too. Looking at QAnon is seeing the advent of a new religion and not just a conspiracy theory.

Many people were hesitant to talk about QAnon with me when I was researching this article. Adherents of the movement have often shown themselves able to take matters into their own hands. The FBI last year classified QAnon in an internal memo as a domestic-terror threat. The memo took note of a California man who was caught with bomb-making materials in 2018. He had intended to strike the Illinois capital to "make Americans aware of 'Pizzagate' and the New World Order (NWO) that were undermining civilization," according to the FBI. The memo also mentioned a QAnon follower in Nevada who was arrested in 2018 after blocking traffic in an armored truck on the Hoover Dam. The guy, heavily armed, requested the publication of a report by the inspector general on emails from Hillary Clinton. The FBI memo cautioned that conspiracy theories fuel the threat of extremist violence, particularly when individuals "claiming to serve as 'researchers' or 'investigators' identify individuals, companies, or groups that they falsely accuse of involvement in the imagined scheme."

Adherents of QAnon are feared online for vicious attacks on skeptics and incitement to physical abuse. Commenters took joy in explaining Clinton's possible fate on a now-defunct Reddit page devoted to QAnon. One person wrote: "I am shocked that no one yet actually murdered her." Another: "Buzzards ripped her rotting corpse to shreds." A third: "I want to see her blood flowing down the gutters!

Recently, when I spoke to Clinton about QAnon, she said, "I'm only getting under their skin unlike everyone else ... If I didn't have Secret Service security getting through my mail, finding weird things, monitoring the threats against me — which are still really high — I'd be concerned." She realized that the imagined world in which conspiracy theorists put her isn't a crazy parallel universe. Referring to internet trolling operations, Clinton said, "I don't think until relatively recently most people have known how well coordinated they were, and how many different components of their plan they put in place."

ON OCTOBER 28, 2017, the now commonly referred to the anonymous user as "Q" first appeared on 4chan, a so-called imageboard notorious for its gruesome images, sickening photos, and violent teardown culture. Q predicted Hillary Clinton's imminent detention and a violent national rebellion, posting this:

successful HRC extradition with many countries in the event of cross-border execution. Authorized passport to be flagged effective 10/30 @ 12:01am. Expect to happen huge defiantly orchestrated protests and others fleeing the US. The operation will be performed by US M's while NG is allowed. Proof check: Locate a member of the NG and ask if it is activated in most major cities for duty 10/30

Then this:

Mockingbird HRC was detained and not (yet) convicted. Where is Huma from? Check-in on Huma. That has (yet) little to do with w / Russia. Why is Potus surrounded by w / Generals? What is Army Intelligence? Why go through the three departments in letters? What case of the Supreme Court allows for the use of agencies formed and authorized by MI v Congressional? Who has absolute authority over our military branches w/o conditions of approval until 90 + in conditions of wartime? What is the Language of the military? Where is AW held? Why? Why? POTUS will not be addressing the nation on tv. To avoid negative optics, POTUS needs to separate itself. POTUS understood that the expulsion of criminal rogue elements was necessary as a first step to freeing and passing legislation. Who is graded as having access to everything? Do you think that HRC, Soros, Obama, etc. have more influence than Trump does? Only imagination. Whoever owns this great land owns the Presidential office. For a moment, they (Democrats and Republicans) had never believed they would lose power. This is not a fight against R v D. Why has Soros recently donated all of its money? Why will he be putting all his money into an RC? 10.30.17 God bless you, fellow Patriots.

Clinton wasn't arrested on October 30, but that didn't stop Q, who kept posting dark forecasts and enigmatic riddles — with prompts such as "Find the reflection inside the castle"—often written in the form of enticing fragments and rhetorical questions. Q made it clear that he wanted people to assume that he was a Q clearance intelligence officer or military official, a degree of access to classified information that involves developing nuclear weapons and other highly confidential content. (I use it because many Q followers do it, while Q remains anonymous — thus "QAnon.") Q's tone is conspiratorial to the point of cliché: "I said so much," and "Follow the money," and "Some stuff must stay secret to the very end."

The global cabal's demise is inevitable, Q prophesies. One of his favorite rallying screams is "Enjoy the show"—a nod to an apocalypse to come.

What might have languished on a single picture board as a solitary screed instead incited fervor? According to Brandy Zadrozny and Ben Collins of NBC News, its popularity has been boosted by many conspiracy theorists whose promotion of Q has, in turn, helped to create their online profiles. By now, almost three years since Q's initial messages appeared, there have been thousands of what its followers call "Q drops"— messages posted by Q to imageboards. To indicate the consistency of his identity over time, he uses a password-protected "tripcode," a sequence of letters and numbers that are accessible to other image-board users. (Q's tripcode has sometimes shifted, causing wild flurries.) As Q has relocated from one picture board to the next — from 4chan to 8kun, finding a safe harbor — QAnon adherents have only grown more devoted. If the internet is a huge rabbit hole containing infinitely recursive rabbit holes, QAnon has found its way down all of them somehow, gulping up theories of lesser conspiracy as it goes.

The QAnon belief system looks something like this in its broadest contours: Q is an intelligence or military source with evidence that corrupt world leaders systematically torture children around the world; the malefactors are rooted in the

Deep State; Donald Trump works relentlessly to foil them. ('These individuals must ALL be Destroyed,' Q wrote in one post.) The complete collapse of the global elite is inevitable, Q prophesies, but can only be done with the help of patriots who seek meaning in the Q's clues. To believe Q demands that conventional institutions be dismissed, government officials ignored, apostates challenged, and the press hated. One of Q's favorite rallying screams is, "You are the news now." Another is "Enjoy the show," a term his followers see as a nod to a coming apocalypse: when the world comes to an end as we know it, everybody is a spectator.i

People who have taken Q to heart like saying they've been paying attention from the very beginning, the way someone might boast about listening to Radiohead before The Bends. A pledge of foreknowledge is part of Q's appeal, as is the feeling of being part of a hidden society, intensified by the use of acronyms and repetitive phrases like "Nothing can stop what's coming" and "Trust the plan."

One sentence that serves as a special touchstone among QAnon adherents is "the calm before the storm." Q first used it a few days after his initial message, and it came with a particular story. On the evening of October 5, 2017—not long before Q first became identified on 4chan — President Trump stood next to the first lady in a loose semicircle of about 20 senior military officers and their spouses for a portrait in the White House State

Dining Room. Reporters had been invited to watch the poses and smiles of Trump's guests. Trump simply couldn't stop talking. "You guys know what that's like? "At one point, he asked to draw an incomplete circle with his right index finger in the air. "Tell us, sir," asked one onlooker. The response from the president was self-satisfied, bordering on a draw: "Maybe it is the calm before the storm."

"Which storm is it? "Asked one of the journalists.

"Maybe the calm before the hurricane," Trump said once more. His repetition was apparently for dramatic effect. Picture shutter whirls got louder.

The reporters got insistent: "Mr. President, what storm? Trump's curt response: "You'll find out."

Those 37 seconds of presidential uncertainty instantly made headlines — relations with Iran had been strained in the last few days — but they would also become fundamental mythology for eventual Q followers.

The circular hand motion of the president is of special interest to them. You may think he was going around him to the semicircle, they say, but he was drawing the letter Q in the air. Was Trump playing John the Baptist's role in announcing what was to come? Was he the anointed One himself?

It is difficult to know with any accuracy the number of QAnon adherents, but the ranks are rising. According to an online tally by the progressive group Media Matters for America, at least 35 current or former Congressional candidates have endorsed Q. These candidates either praised QAnon specifically in public or cited QAnon slogans with approval. (One Republican candidate for Congress, Matthew Lusk of Florida, contains QAnon under the 'issues' section of his campaign page, asking: 'Who is Q?') QAnon has now reached every major social and commercial forum and any range of fringe websites. Tracy Diaz, an evangelist from QAnon, known online as TracyBeanz, has 185,000 followers on Twitter and more than 100,000 subscribers to YouTube. She helped bring QAnon out of the darkness and enabled its introduction to mainstream social media. (A publicist described Diaz as "very private" and refused interview requests.) On TikTok, videos containing the hashtag #QAnon received millions of views. Too many QAnon Facebook groups, many of the ghost towns, are there to do a proper count, but the most popular ones publish thousands of things every day. (Reddit banned QAnon groups from its violence incitement site in 2018)

Adherents are still watching out for signals from on high, plumbing for portents when there is no input from Q itself. For e.g., the coronavirus-what does it mean? In some of the major Facebook groups, people exploded in a whirlwind of speculation, spreading a hypothesis that Trump's decision to wear a yellow tie to a White House briefing about the virus was a sign that the epidemic was not real: "He informs us that there is no virus threat because it is the same color as the maritime flag that represents the vessel that has no infected people on board," someone wrote. Three days before the coronavirus was formally deemed a pandemic by the World Health Organization, Trump was retweeting a QAnon-themed image. "Who knows what that means but to me, it sounds amazing! "On March 8, the president posted a Photoshopped image of himself playing the violin overlaid with the words" Nothing will hinder what is to come.

Q himself released a triptych of ominous posts on March 9 that seemed definitive: The coronavirus is true but welcome, and followers shouldn't be scared. The first post was posted the night before Trump's tweet and echoed, "Nothing Can Stop What Is Coming." The second said, "Worldwide is the Great Awakening." The third was simple: "GOD WINS."

A month later, on April 8, Q went on a posting spree, dropping nine posts over six hours and touching on some of his favorite subjects — God, Pizzagate, and the elite's wickedness. "They'll stop at nothing to reclaim influence," he wrote in one scathing post claiming Democrats, Hollywood, and the media orchestrated propaganda campaigns. Another democrat accused of fostering "mass hysteria" about the coronavirus for political gain: "What is the primary advantage of keeping the mass hysteria republic: COVID 19? Think to vote. Are you still awake? Q. And from Ephesians, he expressed these verses: "Finally, be strong in the Lord, and be strong in His strength. Put on God's full shield, so that you can stand firm against the devil's schemes.

Anthony Fauci, the long-time director of the National Institute for Allergy and Infectious Diseases, has become a target of ridicule among QAnon supporters who don't like the bad news he is providing or the way he openly opposes Trump. Trump referred to the State Department as the "Deep State Department" in one March press conference, and Fauci could be seen over the shoulder of the president, suppressing a laugh and covering up his ears. By then, QAnon had already proclaimed Fauci to be irredeemably corrupted, as, in 2012 and 2013, WikiLeaks had discovered a couple of emails that he sent to laud Hillary Clinton. Feelings about Fauci on social media sites among QAnon supporters range from "Fauci is a Deep State puppet" to "FAUCI is a BLACKHAT!!! "— the term used by QAnon for people who help the evil conspiracy Q warns of. One person tweeted this using the hashtags # DeepStateCabal and # Qanon: "Catching Fauci's hand gestures and body language at the press conferences. How does He communicate? "Another shared with Barack Obama a picture of Fauci standing in a laboratory with the caption "Obama and 'Mr.' Fauci in the laboratory producing coronavirus [sic]. # DeepstateDoctor.

"Recently, the Department of Justice approved heightened security measures for Fauci as threats against him increase.

In the last days before Congress approved a $2 trillion economic-relief bill in late March, Democrats insisted on clauses that would make voting by mail simpler for voters, causing Q itself to weigh in with dismay: "These people are sick! Nothing will hinder what is to come. None at all.'

THE BELIEVERS OF QAnon

On a bone-cold Thursday in early January, in downtown Toledo, Ohio, a crowd swelled up. By lunchtime, seven hours before Trump's first New Year's campaign rally began, the line to join the Huntington Center had already snaked around two city blocks. The air was electric with anticipation, and the whole scene contained an aura of Jimmy Buffett – meets – Michigan Militia: lots of white people, lots of smoking, all red-white-and-blue. Someone had affixed a two-story banner over the top of a burnt-out brick building down the street. It read: PRESIDENT TRUMP, WELCOME TO TOLEDO, OHIO: Who is Q ... INTELLIGENCE MILITARIA? F+? ("Q+" is a QAnon shorthand for Trump himself.) Vendors sold Q buttons and T-shirts at the event. QAnon merchandise comes in a large variety; Great Awakening coffee ($14.99) and QAnon bracelets with tiny silver pizza charms ($20.17) can be purchased online.

Chapter 2: THE INTERVIEW

I worked my way to the back of the line, making small conversations and wondering who knew anything about QAnon if any. One woman's eyes were lit up, and she unzipped and removed her jacket in a single fluid motion, then made a little hop so that her back was to me. I could see a Q made of duct tape pressed onto her red T-shirt. Her name was Lorrie Shock, and the first thing she needed me to remember was the following: "We are not a group of domestic terrorists."

The shock was born in Ohio and never left, as she put it, "a lifer." She'd been working for most of her adult life at a Bridgestone factory, producing car parts. "Real hot and dirty work, but good money," she told me. "I got three kids through school." Today, she looks after adults with special needs in what she calls her pre-retirement career, spending her days in a tender routine of playing games with them and getting them in and out of the pool. Shock and her friend Pat Harger, who had retired in Whirlpool after 32 years, came to the Trump rally. Harger's wife operates a catering company, which is what stopped her from attending that day's rally. Harger and Shock are lifelong friends. "After grade four," Harger told me, "and we are 57."

Now that the girls of Shock are grown and she does not work a factory job, she has more time for herself. That used to mean reading novels at night—she doesn't own a TV—but now it's about studying Q, who first came to her notice when someone she met listed him on Facebook in 2017: "What caught my attention was 'study.' Do your own research. Don't take the matter for granted. And President Trump, I don't care who says it. Do your own study, make your mind up.'

The QAnon universe is vast and broad, with meaning, acronyms, characters, and shorthand to learn layer by layer. The White House is "Home." "Crumbs" are hallmarks. CBTS stands for "the calm before the storm," and WWG1WGA stands for "Where we go one, we go all," which has become a symbol of Q followers' unity. (Both of these terms are strangely used in the trailer for the 1996 Ridley Scott White Squall movie—look at it on YouTube, and you'll see that the comment section is filled with Pro-Q sentiment.) There's also a 'Q clock,' which refers to the calendar used by some Q supporters groups to try and decipher purported clues based on Q drops and Trump tweets.

At the height of her dedication, Shock spent four to six hours a day reading and re-reading Q fall, scouring online papers, taking notes. Ok, she says, she's spending an hour or two a day more. "When I started first, everybody thought I was nuts," said Shock. This included her daughters, who are "really liberal supporters of Hillary and Bernie," Shock said. "I love them anyway. They think I'm mad, but it's okay.

Harger once felt the Shock had lost it, too. "I had reservations about her," he said to me. "I'd send her texts saying, Lorrie."

"He was just saying, 'What the fuck? "She said, shock, laughing. "That will be my response to him, 'Do your own analysis.'"

"And I did," said Harger. "It's like, Wow," he said.

Taking a page from Trump's playbook, Q is always railing as bogus against legitimate sources of information. Shock and Harger rely not on news sources run by journalists but on details they find on Facebook. They neither read the local paper nor watch any of the big TV networks. "You can not look at the television," said Shock. "Your news channel won't tell us shit," says Harger, who likes One America News Network. Not too long ago, he used to watch CNN and couldn't get enough of Wolf Blitzer. "We've always been glued to that; we have always been," he said. "The guy, Trump, really opened our eyes to what's going on. And Q. Q shows us the stuff that will happen beforehand. "I asked Harger and Shock to provide examples of predictions that had come true. They were unable to provide information and instead encouraged me to do my research. When I asked them how they explained the events Q had expected never to have occurred, such as the arrest of Clinton, they said deception was part of Q's strategy. Shock said, "I think it was expected there was more stuff that happened." Her tone was gentle rather than indignant.

"I feel as if God guided me to Q. I feel like God has moved me in this direction.

Harger wanted me to know it was the first time he had voted for Obama. He was born into a Democratic family. His father was a union leader. But that was before Trump emerged, and Harger was persuaded he shouldn't trust the institutions that he once felt he could. Next to him, nodded horror. "The reason I feel more optimistic about Trump is, he's not part of the system," she said. At one point, Harger told me to look at what happened to John F. Kennedy Jr.—who died in 1999 when his aircraft crashed off Martha's Vineyard into the Atlantic Ocean — suggesting that Hillary Clinton had assassinated him. (Alternatively, a group of QAnon believers argues that JFK Jr. fabricated his death and that he was a behind-the-scenes Trump supporter, and probably even Q himself. Some expect his dramatic public return so that he could serve as Trump's running mate in 2020.) When I asked Harger if there was any evidence to support the assassination claim, he turned my question around: "Is there any proof that there is no evidence to support the assassination claim?

Reading Shock's Facebook page is a conflicting practice, a toggling between banality and animosity. In her profile photo, she is in a yellow kayak, bright-red hair streaming out of a ski hat, a huge grin on her face. There are her daughters' pictures and a granddaughter with curls from Shirley Temple.

Nevertheless, Q is never far away. On Christmas Eve, Shock shared one post that seemed to be coming straight out of the QAnon universe but also dragged into an older, classic conspiracy: "X marks the spot over Roswell NM. X17 Fifth Force Particle. Coincidence X + Q? "She posted a different post the same day claiming the Michelle Obama is a man in secret. Someone answered skeptically: "I am still unconvinced. She is demonstrating and behaving badly, but a man? "Shock's reply: 'Study it.' There was a post alleging that Rep. Adam Schiff had raped a dead boy's body at Chateau Marmont in Los Angeles—Harger appears here with a 'huh??' "In the comments — and a note that the Christian evangelicals were going after George Soros. Shock playfully taunted "libs" and her "Trump-hating friends" in other tweets and even posted a video of her daughter singing Christmas carols.

I asked Shock in Toledo if she had any theories about Q's identity. She immediately responded: "I think it's Trump." I asked if Trump thinks she even knows how to use 4chan. For the uninitiated, the message board is notoriously confusing, nothing like Facebook and other social media designed to make fast and regular publishing simple. "I believe he knows much more than we think," she said. But she also wanted me to know that Trump wasn't about their obsession with Q. That was something she had at first been hesitant to talk about. Now she said, "I feel that God has taken me to Q. I always felt as if God had moved me in that direction. I feel like it's deceitful, God will tell me in my mind, 'It is enough.' But I don't feel it. I pray. I hope. I said, 'God, do I need to waste my time on this? '... And I don't believe like I can quit feeling.'

Arthur Jones, the documentary film director Feels Good Man, who tells the story of how internet memes invaded politics during the 2016 presidential election, told me that QAnon reminds him of his childhood growing up in the Ozarks in an evangelical-Christian family. He said that many people he met then, and many people he sees now in the most devoted areas of the world, are profoundly interested in the Book of Revelation and in trying to unpack "all of its pretty-hard-to-decipher prophecies." Jones went on: "I think the same kind of person will suddenly begin to pull Q's threads and begin to feel like something is beginning to fall into place." If you are an evangelical and look at Donald Trump on face value, he's lying; he's stealing, he's cheating, he's married numerous times, he's a sinner. But you're trying to find a way he's part of God's plan in some way.'

You can't tell you what kind of Q follower you're coming across. Anyone who uses a Q hashtag may be a true believer, like Shock, or just someone who cruises a site and plays along for a vicarious thrill. There are people who know that Q is fiction but participate because there is a QAnon aspect that converges with a role-playing live-action game. Shock and Harger appear prototypical in the vast array of Q supporters. They happened on Q and clicked on something. The fable conveniently fitted into its current narrative.

Q MAY BE ANONYMOUS, but QAnon movement pioneers came out in public and built up their broad audiences. By his online username, David Hayes is best known: PrayingMedic. He exudes the even-keeled bureaucratic drive of a middle school principal in his YouTube videos. PrayingMedic is one of the planet's most famous QAnon evangelists. He has over 300,000 followers on Twitter and a large amount of YouTube subscribers. Hayes, a retired paramedic, is living in a terracotta-roofed suburb in Gilbert, Arizona, with his wife Denise, an artist he met at Christian Mingle's 2007 dating site. Both identify themselves as former atheists who came late in life, after previous marriages, to their faith in God and each other. Hayes has been following, or similar to, Q from the beginning. "QAnon is pretty darn interesting," he wrote on December 12, 2017, six weeks after Q's first 4chan message on his Facebook page. He wrote about a sudden call the same day which he felt:

My dreams indicated that God wants me to focus my attention on politics and current affairs. I decided to do a daily news show and current affairs on Periscope, after some prayer. I'm trying to broadcast one single day. (The videos are uploaded to my Youtube channel as well.) That's it.

Hayes is a Q-universe Hero. His "Q for Beginners Part 1" video has been viewed over a million times. "Any of the people following Q will think of themselves as conspiracy theorists," Hayes says in the video. "I don't think of myself as a conspiracy theorist. I consider myself an investigator of the Q. I have nothing against those people who want to pursue the conspiracies. That is their stuff. That's not my material.'

Hayes has built a following partly because of his sheer ubiquity but also because he wears a skeptic's mantle skilfully — I'm not one of those crazies. Hayes, however, is not a hobbyist at QAnon. He's an associate instructor. Earnings sources are to be accessed, small, but growing. On Amazon, Hayes' book Calm Before the Hurricane, the first of what he claims might easily be a "Q Chronicles" 10-book collection, which sells for $15.29. In the introduction, Hayes writes that since 2017 he and Denise devoted their full-time attention to QAnon. "Denise and I were encouraged by those who continued to assist us as we set aside our regular work to study messages from Q," he wrote. He has written several other books giving a peek into an earlier life. The titles include Hearing God's Voice Made Plain, Beating Your Enemy at Heaven's Court, and American Sniper: Spiritual Warfare Lessons. In 2018 Hayes enrolled Praying Medic as a charitable religion in Washington State.

Hayes informs his followers that he thinks Q is an open-source intelligence project made possible by the internet and built within the intelligence community by patriots who combat corruption. Ultimately his understanding of Q is philosophical and relies on the notion of a Great Awakening. *"I think The Great Awakening has a double scope,"* Hayes wrote in November 2019 in a blog post.

It speaks of an intellectual awakening — the public's knowledge of the fact that we were trapped inside a corrupt political framework. But the discovery of the elites' unparalleled depravity could contribute to our depravity becoming more conscious of it. The knowledge of sin itself is a fertile ground for spiritual revival. I believe the spiritual awakening long-prophesied lies on the other side of the wind.

Beyond the largest social media sites and picture boards, the most famous QAnon personalities have a presence. The Q universe contains various blogs, proprietary pages, and chat app styles, as well as alternative social media outlets such as Gab, the forum notorious for anti-Semitism and white nationalism, where many people have gathered forbidden from Twitter. Patreon accounts are sponsored by vloggers and bloggers, where users can pay them in monthly amounts. There's money to be made from YouTube advertising, as well. That seems to be the main priority for Hayes, whose videos were watched more than 33 million times overall. His "Q for Beginners" video contains advertisements from companies such as Vrbo 's holiday-rental platform and the international pro-Trump tabloid, The Epoch

Times. Q evangelists have taken a half marketing, half redundancy strategy to "publishing everywhere." If one forum cracks down on QAnon as did Reddit, they won't have to start somewhere else from scratch. Already entangled in the war between good and evil, QAnon has engaged in another fight — against the notion of an open people's web and a powerful few-controlled gated internet.

WHO ARE Q?

Any NEW BELIEF SYSTEM faces opposition. Matt Patten, a former SWAT-team sergeant at the Broward County Sheriff's Office in Florida, was pictured on an airport tarmac along with vice president Mike Pence in December 2018. Patten wore a patch that bore the letter Q on his tactical vest. The office of the vice president tweeted the photo and then went viral in the QAnon culture. The tweet was taken down quickly. It was demoted to Patten. On a dull day in August, when I knocked at his house, no one replied. But as I turned to go, I saw two huge bumper stickers on the front of the white mailbox. One said TRUMP, and one said # QANON: Battle PATRIOTS.

Q itself lost its forum late last summer. He had moved from 4chan to the imageboard 8chan (fearing the web had been "infiltrated"), and then 8chan went dark. Three days before I stood on the doorstep of Patten, 22 people were killed in a mass shooting at a Walmart in El Paso, Texas, and police announced that the suspected gunman had posted a manifesto on 8chan hours before the attack was carried out. The episode had unsettling resemblances with two other shootings. The alleged gunman in a murderous rampage in a synagogue in Poway, California, had posted an anti-Semitic letter on 8chan four months earlier, in April 2019. The man who killed 51 worshippers at two mosques in New Zealand had posted a white-supremacist manifesto on 8chan weeks earlier.

Jim Watkins, the owner of 8chan, was asked to testify in front of the House Committee on Homeland Security after El Paso. Four years earlier, Watkins had bought the platform from his creator, Fredrick Brennan, now 26, who ultimately cut all ties to 8chan. "This is, regrettably, at least the third act of white nationalist terrorist violence connected to your website this year," wrote Mississippi Democrat Bennie Thompson and Alabama Republican Mike Rogers, when they summoned Watkins to Capitol Hill. "Americans need to know what you, as the owner and developer, are doing to deal with the proliferation of terrorist material on 8chan, if anything."

8chan had already lost key services, which forced her to shut down. Cloudflare's CEO, who helped defend the site from cyberattacks, described his decision to remove 8chan in an open letter after the shooting of El Paso: "The reason is simple: they proved to be lawless, and that lawlessness caused several tragic deaths." Watkins vowed to keep the site off the internet until after his appearance at the Congress. He is an ex-U.S. Army helicopter repairman who got into the website business while still in the army. He opened, among other things, a popular porn site called Asian Bikini Bar in 1997. He regularly chants hymns on his YouTube channel, where he posts under the username Watkins Xerxes, reads verses from the Bible, praises Trump, and touches on the concepts underlying QAnon — warning against the Deep State and reminding his audience members that they are now "the actual reporting tool of the press." He also shows off his array of fountain-pen and yoga activities. In September 2019, when he arrived on Capitol Hill, Watkins was wearing a bulbous silver Q pinned to his chest. His testimony took place behind closed doors. 8chan flickered back to life in November, as 8kun. It was available sporadically, limping through a series of cyber-attacks. It was supported by a Russian hosting service, which is usually synonymous with spreading malware. When Q reappeared on 8kun, he used the same tripcode on 8chan. He posted other clues that were intended to check the consistency of his identity, including a notebook picture and a pen that had appeared in previous posts.

The theory of Fredrick Brennan is that Jim and his son, Ron, who is the administrator of the site, knew that 8kun needed Q to attract users. "I certainly believe 100 percent that Q knows either Jim or Ron Watkins, or that Jim or Ron Watkins is hired," Brennan told me. Both Jim and Ron denied knowledge of Q's identity. "I don't know who Q is," Ron told me via a direct Twitter post. In September 2019, Jim told an interviewee on One America News Network: "I don't know who QAnon is. We're running an anonymous website. "Both say they only care about keeping 8kun because it's a forum for free speech. "8kun is like a sheet of paper, and the users decide what's written on it," Ron told me. "There's a lot of different topics and users from a lot of different backgrounds," he said. Jim launched a super PAC in

February called Disarm the Deep State, which echoes Q's messages and runs paid ads on 8kun.

Brennan has been in rivalry with the Watkins for a long time. In the Philippines, where they both lived until recently, Jim sues Brennan for libel, and Brennan is vigorously battling Jim's attempts to become a naturalized citizen there. "They kept Q alive," Brennan told me. "If Q didn't go on the latest 8kun, we wouldn't be talking about that right now. The main reason we talk about that is that they are directly linked to Q. And, you know, I constantly worry that there will be some kind of shooting or something relevant to Q as early as November 2020 if Trump loses. Or parents kill their kids to save them from the hell-world to come because the Deep State won. Such are real opportunities. I just feel like what they did is completely unethical to keep Q running.

Q's narrative is premised on the need to keep Q secret. That is why Q originally chose 4chan, one of the last places on the social network designed for anonymity. "I have always linked Q to preceding figures like John Titor or Satoshi Nakamoto," Brennan told me, referring to two Internet anonymity legends. The name used by the mysterious bitcoin developer is Satoshi Nakamoto. John Titor is the name that someone appears to be a military time traveler from the year 2036 used on many message boards in 2000 and 2001.

QAnon adherents see Q's anonymity as confirmation of Q's integrity – considering their profound distrust of anonymous media outlets. -- QAnon faction has its hunches, alliances, and interpersonal dramas relating to the Q's identity issue. Three different categories fit into the hypotheses. In the first category are hypotheses suggesting Q is a single person posting all alone this whole time? This is where you can find those people who say Trump is Q himself or even that PrayingMedic is Q. (This category also includes the possibility, posed by people outside QAnon, that Q is a lone Trump supporter who started posting as a form of fan fiction, not realizing it would take off; and the suggestion that Q started posting to mock Trump and his supporters, not expecting people taking him seriously.) This second group involves Brennan's suggestion that the Watkins either pay Q, or pay someone to carry on as Q, or even behave as Q itself. The third group of theories holds that Q is a collective, sharing access to the account with a limited number of individuals. This third category involves the notion that Q is a modern sort of military-intelligence open-source service.

Many QAnon adherents see sense in Trump tweets that contain words beginning with the letter Q. Latest developments around the globe have amply rewarded them. "I am a wonderful Queen & UK friend and admirer," Trump started one tweet on March 29. He had tweeted this the previous day: "I'm contemplating a QUARANTINE." The Q crowd jumped on both tweets, claiming that if you disregard much of the letters in the posts, you'll notice Trump's confession: "I'm ... Q."

REASON VERSUS FAITH

In a Miami coffee shop last year, I met a man who, in recent years, got a whirlwind of attention for his research on conspiracy theories — a professor of political science at Miami University called Joseph Uscinski. I've known Uscinski for years, and his opinions are complex, highly educated, and far from what you'd consider political knee-jerk. Many people believe, he told me that according to ideological lines, a tendency for conspiracy theory is inevitable. This is incorrect, he explained. It is easier to think of conspiracy theories as being independent of political affiliation. It is a specific type of mind- wiring. And it is usually defined by the acceptance of the following propositions: the schemes hatched in hidden places govern our lives. While we technically live in a democracy, all are controlled by a small group of individuals, but we do not know who they are. When big events happen — pandemics, recessions, conflicts, terrorist attacks — it's because the shadowy organization operates against the rest of us.

QAnon isn't a far-right plot, Uscinski continued the way it's sometimes portrayed, despite its pro-Trump narrative. And that is because Trump is not a stereotypical far-right leader. Q appeals to those with the greatest attraction to some form of conspiratorial thought, and that appeal crosses ideological lines.

QAnon carries on an apocalyptic thought tradition that has spanned thousands of years. To encourage those who feel adrift, it provides a polemic.

Some of the people most likely to accept theories of conspiracy see themselves as victims-warriors battling against oppressive and influential powers. They express Corporate elite hate. That helps to understand why populism and conspiracy thought cycles tend to rise and fall together. Conspiracy theory is a trigger at once and a result of what Richard Hofstadter famously described in American politics in 1964 as "the paranoid type." But don't make the mistake of believing conspiracy theories are just scribbled in American history's marginalia. Every big news event they color: John F. Kennedy's murder, the moon landing, 9/11. They also led to enduring profound eruptions like McCarthyism in the 1950s and anti-Semitism at any moment you like. But that is different from QAnon. It may be motivated by fear and racism, but it is also driven by religious conviction. The Q movement has come to describe the language of evangelical Christianity. QAnon marries a conspiratorial appetite with hopeful expectations about a dramatically different and happier future, one that is predetermined.

That was part of the reason why QAnon attracted Uscinski 's mother, Shelly, who was 62. Shelly, who lives in New Hampshire, was searching for videos on YouTube a few years ago — she can't recall what, exactly, maybe a tutorial on how to sparkling-clean her car windows — and the algorithm supported QAnon. She recalls the sense of magnetic attraction. "Wow, what is that, like? "When I talked to her by phone, she remembered. "For me, it exposed certain stuff that I would have hoped would come to pass." She felt that Q understood her anxieties — as if someone were taking her thought train and "actually verbalizing it." Shelly's grievances are wide-ranging and based mostly on the systems that she sees as broken. She has had enough of the school system, the financial system, the newspapers. "And our churches are totally out of whack," she said. His frustration with "the fake news" was one of the items that most resonated with her about Q. She gets her details mainly from Fox News, Twitter, and the New Hampshire Union Chief. "I think things have gotten increasingly worse in my lifetime," said Shelly. Somewhat later, she added: "Q gives us hope. And being optimistic is a good thing.'

Shelly likes Q to quote from scripture sometimes, and she wishes he inspires people to pray. Ultimately, she said, QAnon is about something so much larger than Trump or something else. "There are followers of QAnon out there," said Shelly, "who say that what we're going through now, in this insane political realm we're in now, with all the stuff happening all over the world, is very biblical, and that this is Armageddon."

I asked her if she felt the end of the world was upon us. "It will come as no surprise to me," she said.

Joseph Uscinski 's belief in QAnon disturbs his mother. He doesn't speak easily about it. And Shelly doesn't appreciate the irony of the situation of the family since she doesn't believe that QAnon is, first and foremost, a sort of conspiracy thought. When I referred to QAnon as a conspiracy theory at one point in our conversation, she immediately interrupted: "It's not a theory. It's the foretelling of things to come. "When I asked if she had ever tried to get Joseph to believe in QAnon, she laughed hard. The response was an unambiguous no: "I am his mother, so I love him."

THE APOCALYPSE

In comets and earthquakes, in wars and pandemics, WATCHKEEPERS FOR THE End of Days will quickly find signs of imminent doom. It was always this way. In 1831 a Baptist preacher named William Miller in rural New York started openly expressing his belief that Jesus' Second Coming was imminent. They were finally settled on a date: 22 October 1844. On 23 October, as the sun came up, his followers, known as the Millerites, were killed. The episode will come to be called The Great Deception. Still, they have not yielded. The Millerites became the Adventists, who, in turn, became the Seventh-day Adventists, who now have more than 20 million members worldwide. "These people in the QAnon community — I feel like they're as profoundly misguided, as deeply invested in their convictions as the Millerites were," said Travis View, one of the podcast hosts named QAnon Anonymous, who are subjecting QAnon to acerbic analysis. "This makes me pretty sure that this isn't something that's going to go away with the end of Trump's presidency."

QAnon carries on an apocalyptic thought tradition that has spanned thousands of years. It provides a polemic for motivating those who feel adrift. The historian Norman Cohn explored the evolution of apocalyptic thought over several centuries in his classic 1957 book, The Creation of the Millennium. He found one common condition: This way of thinking had increasingly arisen in regions where the rapid social and economic change took place — and at times when displays of impressive wealth were highly noticeable but inaccessible for most people. This was valid in Europe in the 11th century during the Crusades, and in the 14th century during the Black Death, and in the 16th century in the Rhine Valley, and in the 19th century in New York in William Miller. It's true in 21st century America.

The Seventh-day Adventists and the Latter-day Saints Church of Jesus Christ are flourishing indigenous American religious movements. Do not be shocked if QAnon is turning into another. It now has by far more followers than any of those two religions had in their first decades of existence. People express their faith by the devoted study of Q drops as installments of a foundational text, by forming Q-worshipping groups, and by sweeping expressions of appreciation for what Q has brought to their lives. Is it relevant that we don't even know who Q is? Even the Supernatural is a mystery. Is it relevant that we can not confirm the basic aspects of Q's teachings? There is no proof of the fundamental tenets of Christianity. Among the QAnon people, trust remains absolute. True believers define a sense of rebornness, an everlasting joy to existential awareness. They are sure a Great Awakening is coming. They will wait for deliverance for as long as they have to.

Chapter 3: THE BOOM IN THE CORONAVIRUS CONSPIRACY

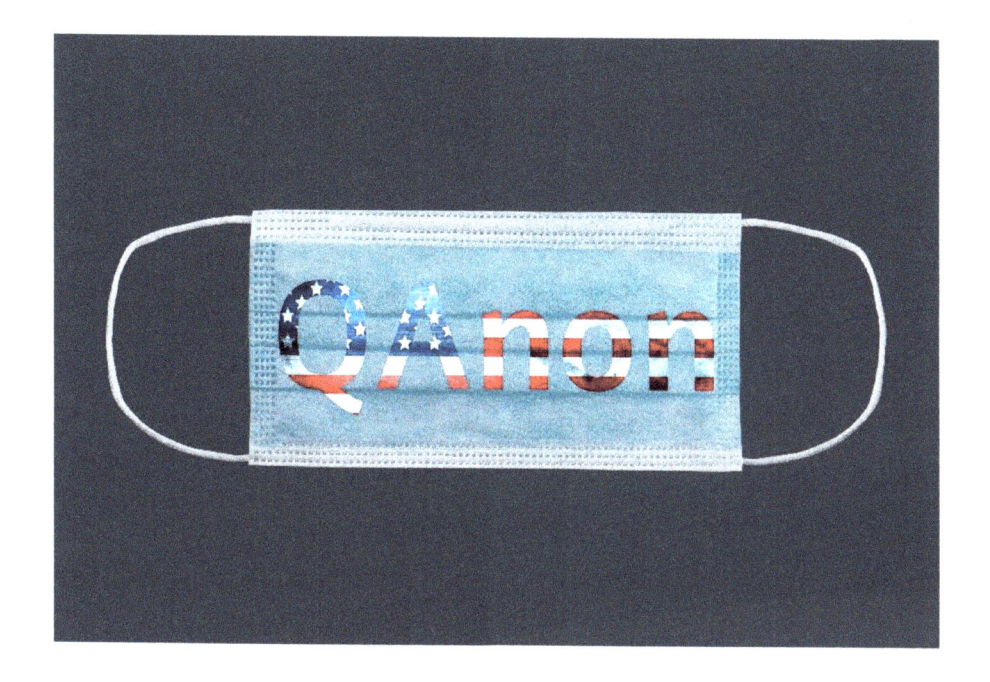

For conspiracy theorists, COVID-19 produced a perfect storm. Here we have a global pandemic, a collapsing economy, social alienation, and restrictive policies of government: all of these can trigger feelings of intense fear, powerlessness, and tension, which in turn promote conspiracy theory. An urban legend that the pandemic was predicted in a Dean Koontz thriller early-'80s has circulated on social media for more than a month. Meanwhile, believers in QAnon are spreading the theory of "mole kids," which holds that the virus is a plot to apprehend members of the satanic "Deep State" (Tom Hanks, Barack

Obama, Hillary Clinton) and free their hostages (sex-slave girls) from underground Central Park. (Tom Hanks' appearance on Saturday Night Live was supposed to have claimed that he was investigated for child molestation, but—in traditional conspiracy fashion—believers merely explained the irregularity away, arguing that Hanks' monolog was a deep-rooted one.)

But if the coronavirus pandemic is a fertile ground for paranoia, it is also an opportunity — a rare chance for social scientists to investigate how many Americans, provided the right set of conditions, would accept conspiracy theories. Although laboratory experiments and public opinion polls are useful in understanding the basic structure of conspiracy ideas, they can not replicate real-world disasters of the sort that cater to certain people to conspiracy theories. It is prudent to step back and use these unusual situations to consider what theories of conspiracy may teach us about the media, the government, and us. It turns out they have a lot to tell us.

Mainstream conspiracy theories about coronavirus come in two varieties: those that dispute the seriousness of the virus and those who say it could be a bioweapon. The former was supported by President Trump, who early in the pandemic referred to the virus as the "latest hoax" of the Democrats. While he has taken the virus more seriously since mid-March, he has yet to expressly denounce the notion of exaggerating the virus' threat or encouraging like-minded leftists to take it seriously in government and media. Indeed, even as the death toll increases, conservative-media figures continue to cast doubt on the truth of the pandemic. For instance, Rush Limbaugh indicated that our officials in public health are deep-state spies and may not even be health experts. The argument has been advanced by some conservative activists that our hospitals do not genuinely treat any COVID-19 patients, going so far as to urge people to stake out local hospitals and record the number of patients going in and out.

The second form of the conspiracy theory of coronavirus argues that the virus was intentionally disseminated in a laboratory by foreign forces, such as China or Russia, or by billionaire philanthropists such as George Soros and Bill Gates. Maybe China developed or operated with this strain of coronavirus, and maybe Gates and the World Health Organization are worried about the virus escaped by mistake. An especially destructive version of this conspiracy theory ties the virus with 5 G technology; in recent weeks, it has motivated believers to destroy cell towers across Europe.

To see how much attention these two core versions of coronavirus conspiracy theories got in the earlier stages of the pandemic, we polled a representative sample of 2,023 Americans from March 17 to 19 on their beliefs in these and several other conspiracy theories. We also questioned survey respondents about their political affiliation and ideological leanings, along with questions designed to capture different worldviews.

The Poll:

Since the pandemic continues to grow and the responses from federal and state governments, we must remember that our findings are just a single snapshot of what we anticipate to be a long time-line. That said, at the onset of the pandemic, when our survey was conducted, conspiracy beliefs about COVID-19 were possibly more prevalent and when social distancing, hand-washing, and other preventive measures. The kinds of behaviors prevented by conspiracy beliefs — had the greatest potential to reduce the spread of the virus. For this reason, our findings are instructive in recognizing the full effect of the prosecutions of coronavirus fraud.

Nearly everyone told us they believe in one of the 22 conspiracy theories we were talking about. Only 9 percent of respondents did not agree with any of the 22. Fifty-four percent believe that the "1%" of the richest Americans secretly run the government. Fifty percent believe that Jeffrey Epstein, a billionaire, was assassinated to mask his activities. Forty-five percent believe that the risks of genetically modified foods are concealed from the public, and 43 percent believe that an extrajudicial Deep State is secretly embedded within our government. Political conspiracy theories — those who specifically accuse one party member of conspiring — often have strong support. Thirty-seven percent of Americans believe Trump has been colluding with Russia to win the 2016 election and that Trump is a Russian weapon. Twenty-eight percent claim that Hillary Clinton sold nuclear weapons to Russia, and 20 percent still claim that Barack Obama fabricated his citizenship to usurp the Presidency illegally.

Meanwhile, 29 percent believe the virus epidemic has been exaggerated to hurt the chances of President Trump's reelection, and 31 percent believe the virus has been created and propagated intentionally. In other words, belief in the theories of coronavirus conspiracy is around in the middle. Around 20 percentage points lower than beliefs in the Epstein and the theories of "1 percent," but about twice as high as beliefs in theories that school shootings are incidents of "false flag," and that the number of Jews killed in the Holocaust has been inflated. Other health conspiracy theories show similar levels of support among the general public: 30 percent believe vaccine risks have been silenced, and 26 percent believe about 5 G technology as much.

These are alarming figures, but, considering what we know about other conspiracy theories, our positive view is that the figures may be much higher. Of course, to monitor the life cycle of these hypotheses as the pandemic progresses, further polling is needed. But, considering America's unparalleled levels of tension, confusion, and impotence feelings, the statistics are likely to suggest a natural limit of conspiracy theories that will be impossible to crack without more prominent figures peddling them.

Where do those convictions come from?

A common belief is that the Internet, and in particular social media, is responsible for the apparent proliferation of conspiracy theories within American political culture. But while these networks make it simpler and more effective to spread every concept, the internet is merely a medium for spreading a human concoction. Social scientists, for the most part, have yet to find proof that conspiracy theories have arisen in the era of the internet. In reality, some conspiracy theories, such as those surrounding the assassination of Kennedy, have lost support as internet access and usage spread. Conspiracy theories also have origins in the basic elements of human psychology and interaction.

The first of those elements is attachments to groups. Simply put, people are inclined to assume that their party is good and right and that bad, evil, or otherwise wrong are other competing groups. People tend to see politics, for example, through their own political or moral lens: their group, their members, and their goals are right, and the other side is inept or corrupt. This dynamic explains why some Republicans assume that Obama "faked" his birth certificate or that Clinton secretly handed uranium to the Russians, just as it accounts for the convictions of some Democrats that Trump is a Russian asset.

These community attachments do not work only from the bottom up. They can be triggered by "cues" from the leaders of their party-speeches, commercials, tweets. If the conspiracy theories are shared by elected officials or media figures affiliated with a political party, their adherents are more likely to take the knowledge to heart and accept certain views. Take the hypothesis that the coronavirus has exaggerated its symptoms to harm Trump. For two reasons, this argument finds considerably more support among Republicans than Democrats: Republicans have more to lose in a presidential election year, and Trump and other right-wing leaders have deliberately peddled the notion that COVID-19 was inflated to benefit him.

The second major causal factor behind the conspiracy theories is "conspiracy theory," a mentality that predisposes people to perceive events and facts as the result of dark conspiracies. When activated — by knowledge implying a conspiracy, or by the rhetoric of political insiders, or by the fear brought on by an uncontrollable disaster — this latent predisposition renders conspiracies an appealing explanation for unexpected circumstances. We tested conspiracy thinking in our poll by asking respondents to react to statements like "The people who really 'run' the country are not known to the electorate." We found that respondents who agree with feelings like this appear to believe more conspiracy theories, deeper. Indeed, our measure of conspiracy thinking highly predicts belief in any of the 22 particular conspiracy theories for which we asked the respondents. It's disturbing, on the one hand, that certain people follow the conspiracy theories so easily. On the other hand, many people don't — and these people serve as a shield to spread myths of conspiracy, losing much of the natural ceiling.

Conspiracy theory is the most predictive of beliefs in particular conspiracy theories, when party figures are not staking out positions and the least predictive when they do. For example, Republican leaders have long challenged the validity of climate change, so much so that they call it a hoax. In this situation, in justifying skepticism of climate change, Republicanism is almost as predictive as a conspiracy theory. But this is not the case for conspiracy theories not dragged into the political arena, such as those about AIDS, vaccines, and genetically modified foods. If theories like these became fodder for common political and ideological leaders, beliefs in them might grow very fast.

The nature of COVID-19 conspiracy theories — how common they are, where they come from, and what they may mean — is entirely predictable within this system. In the case of coronavirus, the main difference is the stakes. For example, we have little reason to be worried about the one in three Americans who believe aliens have made secret contact with humans. And our country was not in danger at any point because almost 80 percent of Americans once felt that the Warren Commission was incorrect with the specifics of the assassination of John F. Kennedy. But the implications of blaming the appearance of the coronavirus on the wrong cause or of doubting its severity, may be significantly life-threatening. People who assume the virus is a bioweapon may have a greater risk of engaging in hoarding and other self-centered behaviors. And if the one in three Americans who think COVID-19's effects have been exaggerated chose to forgo critical health habits, such as social distancing, regular hand-washing, and wearing a mask, then the disease could spread faster and further than otherwise and cost several thousands of lives.

Chapter 4: TECHNOLOGY AND COVID 19

These new technologies and strategies pose a potentially significant threat to the interests of the US and its allies. Yet democracies also fail to interpret knowledge as a potential tool. Many democratic systems have the inherent presumption that the free flow of knowledge is an unalloyed social good. This presumption is not fully undermined by the reality of aggressive actors in the infosphere. Still, it does mean that the United States and other democratic countries need to start thinking more strategically about the knowledge environment, its weaknesses, and also potential benefits.

A POLLUTED ATMOSPHERE

Although there is no definitive proof yet about the implications of what has taken place thus far, these technologies and strategies are symptomatic of genuinely profound changes in open societies' character of the infosphere. The United States urgently needs to work to ensure that foreign powers can not easily manipulate elections or cause major social tensions. But this research points to a much larger task: understanding whether current developments in the infosphere risk are creating conditions that can have serious long-term effects on those societies' cohesion and stability.

This danger may be called infosphere corruption. Usually, the target of aggressors using psychological manipulation tactics won't be to alter fundamental beliefs or vast populations "brainwash." Everything we know about perceptions, shifting behaviors, and persuasion indicates that — unless a manipulator can exert near-total control of a knowledge space — such fine-tuning of beliefs across entire populations is extremely hard. Social manipulators would often attempt to create disruption and conduct a systemic bullying campaign, often involving indirect or even direct physical aggression toward perceived opponents.

These developments in the process will drastically shift our understanding of the influence of authoritarian regimes on world politics. Such states will continue to pursue an iron grip on their own communities' knowledge flows, values, and attitudes, a challenge now driven by the large quantities of data accessible from state-controlled social media networks and surveillance technologies and techniques of the 21st century. But they will also gradually attempt to achieve global scope for some of the components of this autocratic program: not regulating information flows per se, but undermining the free world's confidence in common facts and reality; working hard to deepen social tensions within democracies; and, most of all, resuming an ongoing campaign of abuse, bullying, and virtual and physical violence They would try to provoke the same uncertainty, apprehension, and self-censorship among opponents globally as they do within their borders amongst their people.

Moreover, as multiple states conduct such campaigns, the incremental emergence of a new global alliance — informal but significant — of autocratic states working to subvert the free sphere of knowledge and destabilize democratic societies may be a related risk. Evidence of Russian and Venezuelan collaboration in intervening in the Catalan-Independence debate in Spain has already emerged. Some social media websites in China reposted Russian propaganda.

Over time, countries like Russia, China, Venezuela, Iran, North Korea, and others have been able to find ways to work together to create new information structures, encourage counter-narratives, and achieve unique disruptive impacts. One related outcome may be the deep division of global knowledge networks into overlapping, mutually exclusive regions, including the internet itself, with profound effects on world politics and international relations. This process is already well underway with the efforts of several countries, especially China, to create what amounts to parallel internets.

The full implications of those possibilities are too early to grasp. Liberal democracies have regarding the exchange of information and expertise as a competitive advantage.

"Some people say that there is no coronavirus and there is no risk. But that all of it is orchestrated by some global powers that are involved in pressuring people to reserve and then irradiate them from 5 G antennas to lose consciousness and then implant them with microchips," TASS quoted Bitarov as saying. "There are plenty of people who think so."

Leader of North Ossetia Vyacheslav Bitarov addresses people opposing the April 20 lockdown of coronavirus in Vladikavkaz.

Such baseless claims build on and deepen existing government public mistrust of health and safety matters. And during the current global health crisis, they are especially insidious, as they threaten to drown out important, science-based knowledge about the deadly COVID-19 pandemic and how to effectively combat coronavirus spread.

Any correlation between 5 G technology and COVID-19 is "total nonsense," Simon Clarke, a University of Reading associate professor of cellular microbiology, told the BBC. Stephen Powis, the UK's National Health Service's medical officer, said the allegations of a connection are "the worst kind of false news."

THE ORIGIN STORY

The Cellular-network infrastructure of the fifth-generation (5 G) started to be deployed internationally in 2019. It promises greater bandwidth and data transfer much quicker, up to 10 gigabits per second — or around 100 times quicker than current 4 G technology.

However, this is done by using a radio frequency higher than that of 4 G networks. Some of the used frequencies fly just around 1.6 kilometers and have difficulty reaching certain building materials. Consequently, a 5 G network needs a much denser antenna deployment. As of April 2019, operators had started implementing 5 G technology in 88 countries.

Nevertheless, anti-5 G groups started emerging on social media almost instantly. For example, people posted fake photographs of radiation-warning signs allegedly attached to 5 G antennae. Unfounded and dismissed rumors ran wild that the device was causing cancer or mental illness, killing trees and animals, and so forth.

The anti-5 G movement found willing supporters in the greater movement of citizens who reject all forms of compulsory vaccines — anti-vaxxers — and the movements practically fused in many countries, such as Romania.

Small demonstrations have been seen all over the world.

Protesters raise banners against the 5 G technology and vaccines during an anti-government rally in Sofia, Bulgaria, on May 14.

A May 2019 report in The New York Times reported that RT America, the US-funded Russian state-sponsored broadcasting network, had released one anti-5 G story in 2018. Still, seven in the first four months of 2019, including one alleging children, were especially vulnerable to cancer and other illnesses allegedly caused by 5 G radiation.

"Hundreds of blogs and websites tend to pick up 5 G alarms [RT's], rarely if the Russian roots are ever found," the Times article argued. "Analysts call it a ghastly fog."

The International Commission for the Protection of Non-Ionizing Radiation (ICNIRP) conducted a long-running study that concluded that there are no health hazards associated with the types of radio wave radiation used by 5G.

Came Coronavirus

With the outbreak of the global COVID-19 pandemic in early 2020, various baseless conspiracy theories tried to relate the virus to 5 G technology. Some have suggested that 5 G radiation has damaged the immune system and made people susceptible to the disease. Others went further and said 5 G signals transmitted the virus. Some, like Moldova's Orthodox Church, argued that the 5 G technology and a subsequent coronavirus vaccine were part of a huge conspiracy of mind control.

A variety of celebrities have shared the false allegations on their social media accounts, including actor Woody Harrelson, boxer Amir Khan, television personality Amanda Holden and others. Some have erroneously reported that there are hidden images of a 5 G tower and the coronavirus in a new version of Britain's 20-pound note.

According to Swedish data firm Earhart Market Security Agency, such disinformation, which has been called "the coronavirus infodemic," spread like wildfire. Earhart monitored 35 of the most common 5G-coronavirus videos that appeared on social media in January and found they were viewed almost 13 million times within weeks. TikTok's successful video-sharing application has emerged as a "very powerful tool" that targets younger audiences, the study found.

The false reports sparked a global vandalism campaign against 5 G antennas, and artifacts were assumed to be linked to 5 G networks. In the UK, more than 70 5 G masts were damaged or lost. The Department of Homeland Security released an alert in the United States that such conspiracy theories linking 5 G and COVID-19 are "inciting attacks on the communications infrastructure."

"Violent extremists have benefited from online disinformation campaigns alleging that wireless infrastructure is detrimental to human health and leads to the spread of COVID-19, culminating in a global initiative by like-minded individuals to share operational advice and justification for attacks on 5 G infrastructure, some of which have already triggered explosive and physical attacks on cell towers in

In a study in April, StratCom, the European Council's task force on misinformation within the European Union and its neighborhood, reported that such conspiracy theories had reached 'fertile soil in the Western Balkans, where misinformation has spread on social networks and portals that the 5G network is triggering the [COVID-19] pandemic.'

Chernobyl Disease

The World Health Organization (WHO) and others reacted by vigorously countering the 5 G misinformation. As with other fact-checking organizations, the WHO has built a page on its website dedicated to debunking 5 G conspiracies. For example, the British fact-checker Full Truth frequently reviews false 5 G statements.

However, such unfounded conspiracy theories also gain traction in the areas of health and safety due to increasing public distrust on the part of governments. The anti-vaccination measures have manipulated and bred such mistrust.

The 5 G conspiracy theories seemed to be supported by Nobel Prize-winning Belarusian author Svetlana Alexievich in a recent interview with RFE / RL.

The pandemic, she said, "is the greatest threat since Chernobyl," referring to the 1986 accident and meltdown at Ukraine's Chernobyl nuclear power plant, then part of the Soviet Union. "It remains to be seen if this is flu or whether 5 G affects the human immune system. Scientists, in my view, have no definite conviction."

While any credible scientific research has proven none of the conspiracy theories regarding 5 G and coronavirus, Alexievich 's analogy with Chernobyl is valid.

This incident has become recognized as an example of government indifference to public health, as the Soviet government has, for weeks, obscured the scale of the tragedy and exposed its people to grievous immediate and long-term health risks. It is an example often cited by 5 G conspiracy theorists — along with others such as the 1950s and 1960s thalidomide case and the Tuskegee syphilis experiment — while arguing that governments can not be trusted.

The Maximum Fact-checking website has concluded that "only asking Internet companies to remove this material is not an appropriate solution in a free society, is unlikely to succeed and could even make things worse."

"People are understandably frightened, anxious, and confused, and in any response, we must take that into account," the website concluded. "Not everyone will be convinced. Some people may like conspiracy theories and may not be persuaded by the truth. But because the doubts surrounding 5 G have reached the mainstream, it is up to all of us to address these claims head-on with straightforward, high-quality evidence to reassure those who have questions and concerns, rather than simply dismiss them as stupid."

COVID-19 is a severe, infectious disease caused by a newly discovered coronavirus that originated in late 2019 in Wuhan, China. The virus is transmitted mainly by saliva droplets or a scattered nasal discharge when an infected person coughs or sneezes. According to the Coronavirus Information Center at Johns Hopkins University, as of May 31, there were more than 6 million recorded coronavirus infections worldwide and more than 365,000 fatalities.

THE 5 G CONSPIRACY

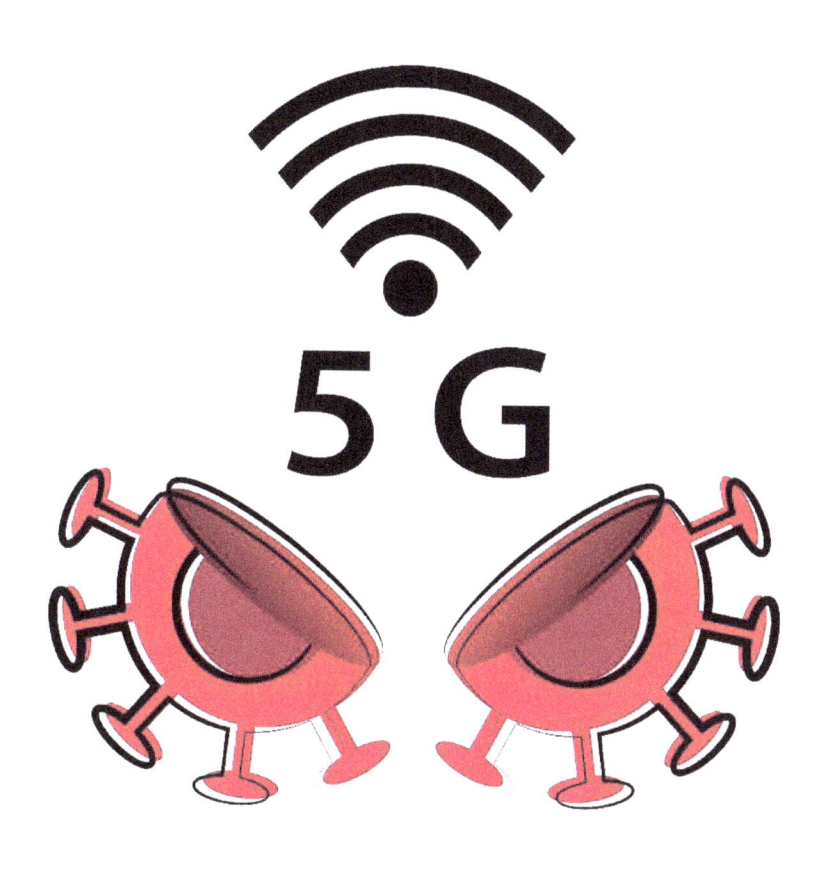

5 G is the latest generation of cellular network infrastructure to be phased out gradually around the United States and the world. It offers higher data rates and network bandwidth than the current 4 G LTE technology, which is expected to allow for new technologies such as smart cities, which robotic surgery.

To understand why a small number of people freak out about it, it's time for a little jargon: At its heart, 5 G is a collection of technical standards that a subset of wireless radio frequency spectrum devices use to connect with the mobile network. It's the same way that 3 G and 4 G operated, with 5 G devices being able to reach a broader spectrum of radiofrequency waves than ever before, allowing for speed and bandwidth improvements.

There are three different types of 5 G networks: networks that use the radio frequency spectrum low-band, mid-band, and high-band. Low-band networks offer extensive coverage, but only minor performance increases, mid-band networks balance capacity and coverage, and high-band networks offer superfast speeds, but signals are not going very far.

Low- and mid-band networks are ultimately expected to reach a significant part of the world. High-band networks would often be established in cities because they need several small-cell sites to be located in a given region to make up for the fact that signals fail to fly.

DEBUNKING THE 5G CONSPIRACY

Many conspiracy theories about 5 G's risks concentrate on the radio frequencies through which signals fly. Yet analysts point out that 5 G networks with low-band and mid-band run at nearly the same frequencies as existing networks.

"In terms of penetration, there is nothing different," said Kenneth Foster, professor of bioengineering at the University of Pennsylvania, whose research focuses on the health and safety implications of electromagnetic fields that interfere with human bodies.

Thanks to high-band networks, where signals stream over millimeter-wave frequencies, big developments from 5 G can come in.

But millimeter-wave frequencies can elicit even less worry, said NYU's Collins because they can't penetrate structures like walls, trees, or human skin (that's one of the reasons they're not traveling very well).

"It's a bit ironic that all this concern about 5 G persists because the difference is that 5 G will be working at higher frequencies," Collins said. "In truth, it won't penetrate as deeply into the body … it doesn't even get through the skin."

People are also familiar with millimeter-wave frequencies in other systems, including airport safety scanners.

"If you are aware of these airport scanners, mmWave energy is being used," Collins said. "You know it doesn't enter the body because the outside surface of the body is what you see in the picture on the screen."

Is there anything of which to worry? The short reply is No.

Like FM radio waves and visible light, radiofrequency waves are a type of "non-ionizing" radiation, meaning they don't have enough energy to destroy the DNA within cells and cause cancer, unlike X-rays, for example. Decades of studies indicate that the only way wireless technology can communicate with the body is by heating the skin, but power levels are so low there's no problem, expert.

What is it that governments do?

Like government agencies elsewhere, the US Federal Communications Commission controls the exposure levels of radio frequencies from cellular devices such as mobile phones. Exposure levels from 5 G radio frequencies fall far below the agency's limits.

"The weight of scientific evidence has not effectively associated exposure from mobile devices to radiofrequency energy with any established health conditions," the FCC states on its website.

YouTube seeks to restrict the spread of bogus 5 G coronavirus stories after targeting cell phone towers

Currently, some critics contend that there have been very few studies on the possible consequences of 5G. In response, most government agencies have emphasized that they will continue to track 5 G research as network technology grows.

"We need to see first how this new technology can be implemented and how the scientific evidence can develop," said Vytenis Andriukaitis, head of the Cabinet of the European Commission. In a 2017 response to critics who asked the Commission to place the 5 G rollout on hold over concerns about potential health effects.

"Be assured that to safeguard the welfare of European citizens at the highest possible stage, the Commission will keep abreast of potential developments," Andriukaitis said.

Foster said such a response to concerns over 5 G is the best possible course of action.

"We can only defend against the hazards that we know exist," said Foster. "The EU approach is as good as you can get — if anything suggests a fair concern, well, then we'll look at the literature."

Uncertainty also gives rise to speculative and ludicrous arguments. Pair it with social media, and you've got a great formula for hackneyed viral statements. As the world fights coronavirus and COVID-19 pandemic, thousands of social media users, conspiracy theorists yes. The kind of people who believe the earth is flat and that moon landings never occurred, say that Microsoft co-founder Bill Gates, who also happens to be the second-wealthiest person, in the world, is behind the development of coronavirus and COVID-19 pandemic.

Why helped Bill Gates create coronavirus? There are several statements, each more terrible than the other. And it would have been easier to ignore them all if they were not trending in a major way on social media and if mainstream figures did not support them.

THE Bill GATES' CONSPIRACY THEORY

The conspiracy theorists have claimed that Bill Gates has created a vaccine that would govern the planet through a microchip and even depopulate it. A Mysterious Times article in 2018 misquoted Gates and said he'd proposed a scheme to depopulate the world. "No mistake, when Gates speaks about 'making us safe,' what he's talking about is simply implementing the mandatory rollout of his collection of experimental vaccines. The same vaccinations already causing mass sterilization and death on several continents, "reported the website.

Gates also warned the world of a pandemic in a TED talk in 2015. He said there would be a pandemic in the next decade, and the pandemic could kill more than 30 million people in six months, similar to the 1918 pandemic that killed more than 50 million people. "The world needs to prepare for pandemics in the same serious way it prepares for war," he said.

While Gates in his TED talk about a pandemic is real for someone interested in public health programs, talking about catastrophic pandemics is fairly normal and simple, all that speaks about the vaccine with microchips is bunkum.

Unfortunately, people are connecting the talk Gates gave to coronavirus, which isn't even a brilliant insight because it's pretty common knowledge that pandemics from unknown viruses are the greatest challenges facing humanity.

Of late, this connection has led to numerous posts on Facebook, alleging that a research institute was funded by Gates and helped to develop the novel coronavirus. A Humans Are Free article reported that Gates worked with research institutes to develop a "weaponized viral strain engineered to sell more ineffective, deadly vaccines while killing some thousand, or even a few million, people at the same time."

Apart from the crowd that claims shape-shifting lizards control the planet, some popular commentators support the theories that say Bill Gates developed coronavirus so that he can be some kind of mind-controlling crazy billionaire. The White House reporter Emerald Robinson has written a series of tweets accusing Gates. She wrote, "The more you research this virus, the more you find the same name: Bill Gates. He is WHO's 2nd largest funder. He's building seven vaccine labs. Fauci. Tedros. Event 201. ID2020. He essentially regulates global health policy. What's the plan?

The theories that Bill Gates has Linked to coronavirus and that he wants to take advantage of the pandemic by promoting some vaccinations that will monitor people have spread via videos on YouTube, Facebook, Twitter, and sites such as InfoWars.

Meanwhile, Gates has called the claims made. In an interview with a China-based news channel CCTV, he said: "I would say it's ironic if you take someone who is trying their best to get the world ready. We're in a crazy situation, so there'll be wild rumors."

"The Bible says there will be an Antichrist, a man who claims to be God, who will attempt to unite the world in a one-world government with a one-world financial system and create a one-world religion," says Pastor Adam Fannin, a notorious Florida preacher. He has latched to the anti-vaccination movement in a recent YouTube video.

Who is this "king who claims to be God?" Fannin refers to Microsoft founder and prominent philanthropist Bill Gates, who has become the latest victim of conspiracy theorists and fringe groups opposing vaccination.

Gates, who has long predicted that the U.S. will not be prepared for a devastating pandemic, has been extremely active since the emergence of the coronavirus, donating $250 million towards the crisis, sponsoring the importance of developing a safe and effective vaccine, and supporting the establishment of government-funded manufacturing infrastructure, but disinformation providers tell a different story,

He lambastes Gates for promoting vaccination in Fannin's video, which has received 1.8 million views, and indicates that he is working on implantable devices with "digital certificates" and "quantum dot tattoos" that would label people with COVID-19 and send their details to the UN. He goes on to name

Antichrist Gates. He makes misleading statements about vaccines in Fannin's other videos, including that they are "loaded with toxic chemicals and aborted fetuses."

Fannin also says that Gates wants to "depopulate" the planet with vaccination, a misconception that has been around for at least ten years. Gates said, as Snopes describes, he sees reducing population growth as a key component of helping to raise people out of poverty—one of his philanthropic initiatives' goals. In addition to promoting progressive policy programs and accessibility to birth control, Gates also supports compulsory vaccination as a way to reduce rates of infant mortality. He assumes that as infant mortality rates decline and stabilize, parents will opt to have fewer children, so their children will die less worried.

Fannin's references to "quantum dot tattoos" are linked to research sponsored by the Gates Foundation. Researchers at the Massachusetts Institute of Technology announced in December the creation of invisible ink, which could be rubbed on the skin of children as a record of their injection at the time of vaccination. The stamp will last for five years, but it's just a stamp. As FactCheck.org states, this can not be used to track a person's whereabouts.

As for the "digital certificates" and implantable devices, Gates has no plans to develop any technology with COVID-19 that would diagnose and monitor individuals. This conspiracy theory seems to come from a Reddit AMA, where Gates noted that we would have digital certificates at some stage that would be able to monitor who was sick, who was vaccinated, and who should receive a vaccine. But Gates' words were distorted to make it look as if he had plans to sell an invasive method of mass surveillance of the population.

Population management is a very controversial issue, particularly for disease control, and one that many people are paying attention to. Doctors also monitor individual human health via electronic health records, and departments of human resources will begin monitoring the health of workers as people return to work. Apple and Google announced a proposal to build a Bluetooth-based, privacy-focused framework to monitor people's exposure to COVID-10, and similar solutions have been proposed by organizations such as MIT. But a Pew Research poll shows that 60 percent of Americans are doubtful that using cell phone data to track people who have come into touch with someone optimistic about COVID-19 would do a lot to delay the virus's spread. People also disagree on whether this form of digital contact tracking should be performed at all—61% of Democrats felt it was appropriate to monitor the movement of the disease this way. In comparison, only 45% of Republicans thought the same thing.

There are also more conspiracies around Gates, including one that claims that he initiated the coronavirus or that he knew it was coming. A New York Times report reported a cache of 16,000 Facebook posts about Bill Gates with 900,000 likes and comments; youTube conspiracies by Bill Gates showed equally strong commitment. Gates has been the subject of conspiracy theories for a long time — like this one from 1996, which says that Microsoft is the Illuminati's invention or that one which suggests that Gates invests in antivirals as a way of colonizing Africa. For at least a decade, radical conspiracy theorists like Alex Jones have argued that Gates is using vaccines to "sterilize" and "depopulate" the world.

What is interesting is how such conspiracy theories – particularly those with an anti-vaccine agenda – can increase on the web. Google (the parent company of YouTube) and Facebook have attempted to take down content that would cause someone to get injured. But videos such as the collapse of Adam Fannin into a category of misinformation not known to be particularly harmful to human health.

"We have straightforward policies, and, when flagged at us, we quickly delete videos that breach those policies. We are those recommendations for borderline content, such as the videos submitted by Fast Business, "a spokesperson for YouTube said. They also noted that most of the 1.8 million views didn't come from site reviews, meaning that YouTube doesn't send people to the Fannin video. Instead, other websites guide viewers to that location.

Yet YouTube is hosting misinformation about health. Although the company has made attempts to steer viewers into trustworthy material, it still leaves gaps to exploit for anti-vaxxers.

Chapter 5: SOCIAL MANIPULATION

Since I've been in self-isolation in the past two weeks, not a single morning has passed that I haven't received a rumor, hoax, and even unprecedented self-created suspicions or conspiracy theories related to the coronavirus pandemic.

Every day I'm bombarded with lies spewing messages from WhatsApp, like this is a biological war or people in power want to govern the population, exploit their resources, and destroy the elderly and weak. Not only do I receive these texts, but all kinds of fearsome and groundless assumptions.

As I write this book, the coronavirus is currently the single most Googled word. Chelsey Needham, one social media user, wrote, "People are stuck in terror and confusion," and that's understandable living under the threat of a killer virus.

Before passing on the incurable poisonous virus of disinformation to another human, thousands of social media users don't even bother with fact checks.

Why do people act so irresponsibly? Should our governments fix such catastrophic blunders?

Despite such reckless conduct on the part of many users, it would be unreasonable to blame social media only for spreading fear-mongering with baseless and venomous COVID-19 details.

At this point, what do we need? Firstly, it is not to fan the fear of hopelessness, as resilience is desperately needed to improve the morale of people to face and defeat the virus.

Should we take any responsibility for social media users? How do we stop the spread of lies on social media? Should we ignore this or report it to the authorities concerned?

Anyway, those who spread deceptive COVID-19 details need to reconsider: are you helping people living in depression? Just think about it.

A while ago, on Facebook, Twitter, YouTube, and WhatsApp, a common self-manufactured hypothesis went viral that Charles Lieber, a professor at Harvard, is behind the research and export of the Chinese killer virus. Isn't that nonsense? Can any nation purchase a killer virus? Is that credible?

Chayan Kundu investigated Lieber's arrest and concluded that in January of this year, he was arrested "for lying and making false claims" to the US authorities about a financial link with Chinese officials. Ok, I'm not a fan of conspiracy theories, but not one single thought penetrates our mobile phones, laptops, iPods, and tablets.

In Britain, where thousands of doctors and nurses have sacrificed their lives to encourage others to live, a WhatsApp message is circulating that says: "Don't go to the hospitals. They inject poison into frail elderly people.' Is this true? What could be worse than sick thinking like this?

Some people say protests are around the corner, so food shortages will arise. Most of the food shortages is merely a manmade political event. Remember the famines in Ireland and Bengal?

So why are people so confident about the infiltration of COVID-19 conspiracy theories? Well, behind the bogus inflow of the myths about the virus, there are some obvious reasons.

Whose incentive is that?

One of the factors that caused concerns about COVID-19 among social media users is the American sitcom show, "The Simpsons." The Daily Mirror reported that fans of the program point to parallels between a 1993 episode of the show named "Marge in Chains" and the current outbreak. Several British newspapers wrote articles about "The Simpsons."

Not only this, but people on social media platforms, including Facebook, Twitter, YouTube, Snapchat, and blogs, are also talking about movies, dramas, novels, and academic articles.

CNN analyst Brian Lowry says that many Hollywood films- including "Contagion," "The Omega Man," "World War Z," and "Pandemic"-all have "potentially unusual parallels with current events."

The next most widely circulated reference to the current COVID-19 outbreak on Facebook and WhatsApp is Dean Koontz's novel, "The Eyes of Darkness," in which the "Wuhan-400" virus is described as "a perfect weapon."

To be honest, numerous newspaper articles and university inquiries have posted self-appointed experts and scholars on new media that distort the original writings, such as The Independent's report, "Fake Bill Gates Letter circulated as COVID-19 misinformation." Fortunately, new media owners and independent organizations such as News Guard are in action to stop distorted and fake news stories.

The British newspaper The Guardian has learned that YouTube's video center would restrict the conspiracy theories that link "5 G technology to coronavirus."

On the other hand, Twitter has a hashtag # conspiracy theories that carry photos, short video clips, and coronavirus adages. Twitter seems to have become a forum for disseminating such collusions.

YouTube is yet another place apart from Twitter and Facebook that has turned out to be a forum for conspiracy theories about coronavirus. One hypothesis asks: "Is it a Chinese bio-warfare weapon?" Well, Dr. Gerald Parker and Professor Andrew S. Natsios are speaking to experts on the subject until you make up your mind.

YouTube also serves as a hub of knowledge for good. But the propagation of positivity involving the coronavirus will be unreasonable to discredit. The same channels also include how to treat infection, treatments, precautions, and drugs.

But if these hypotheses promote our ability to defeat the coronavirus, a key question is. What are you thinking? Why are all of us paying more attention to speculation and taking less account of the facts?

The report by Gouri Sharma carries the judgment of the top 27 scientists from eight countries in the world who condemn the misinformation surrounding the virus and refute the spread of conspiracy theories. These scientists are right to suggest that such thoughts could do nothing but "build uncertainty, speculation, and prejudice that undermines our global cooperation in combating this virus."

Several research institutions have clarified that the coronavirus family was described during the 1960s, named for the "crown-like spikes" on their exterior.

Chapter 6: THE ALLEGATIONS AGAINST QAnon

Why is it so important?

There's no question that the charges are devastating and harmful. But there are plenty of malicious and dangerous allegations floating around the internet, many of which go unnoticed.

For a few important reasons, QAnon is more dangerous: the very misleading accusations it makes are being transmitted to many people, many of whom do not know that they are fak. It bears many parallels to Pizzagate, which ended in real violence when a person entered a pizza restaurant with a weapon.

An FBI intelligence newsletter last year indicated that followers could pose a threat to domestic terrorism. Although certain acts of violence allegedly influenced by QAnon have been taking place, for the time being, they were mainly minor and committed by what appears to be a small minority of adherents of the theory.

In July 2020, Twitter said it would stop promoting QAnon content and accounts in a move that it predicted would affect some 150,000 accounts. It also said it would block QAnon URLs and permanently suspend QAnon accounts, which organize harassment or violate its rules.

In August, Facebook suspended nearly 800 QAnon groups for posts that promoted abuse, displayed intent to use weapons, or attracted followers with trends of violent behavior. It has also placed limitations on the remaining 1,950 QAnon public and private groups identified by it. Facebook said it plans to prohibit advertising supporting or mentioning QAnon, and it does not allow QAnon pages to operate business stores.

A spokeswoman for TikTok's short-form video app said QAnon content "frequently includes misinformation and hate speech" and removed hundreds of hashtags from QAnon.

A Reddit spokeswoman told Reuters that since 2018 when she took down forums such as r / great awakening, the site has deleted QAnon communities, which have repeatedly violated its rules.

A spokesperson for YouTube said she has deleted tens of thousands of Q-related videos and terminated hundreds of Q-related channels for breaching her rules after updating her policy on hate speech in June 2019.

YouTube also said it is that its recommendations for some QAnon videos that "could misinform users in negative ways." It has no clear ban on monetizing QAnon material. ISD researchers found that about 20 percent of all Facebook posts related to QAnon featured ties to YouTube.

Reviews on major Amazon.com Inc and Etsy Inc e-commerce sites show retailers selling QAnon-branded products ranging from books to T-shirts and face masks.

The senior pastor of Round Grove Baptist Church in Miller, Missouri, Mark Fugitt, recently sat down to count the conspiracy theories people in his church post on Facebook. The list had been a long one. It included reports that 5 G radio waves are being used to manipulate the mind. That the murder of George Floyd is a hoax; that Bill Gates is connected to the devil; that masks can destroy you; that the theory of germs is not real; and that after all there may be anything to Pizzagate.

"You just don't see this often," Fugitt said. "If it is ever released, you can see it five to ten times. That's sure to escalate."

Theories of conspiracy. Great theories aimed at showing that influential forces are secretly manipulating events and structures for sinister purposes — are nothing new in the U.S. But a sort of ur-conspiracy theory, QAnon, has merged in online forums since 2017 and has produced millions of believers. "Seeing QAnon is seeing not only a conspiracy theory but the emergence of a new religion," Adrienne LaFrance wrote in June in The Atlantic.

Named after "Q," who anonymously posts 4chan on the online message board, QAnon says that President Donald Trump and military officials are trying to uncover a pedophile "deep-state" network with ties to Hollywood, the media, and the Democratic Party. The theory has attracted adherents since its first mention some three years ago, in search of a straightforward way to describe recent disorienting global events.

QAnon is no longer radical, but the obsession of far-right activists and their supporters. It has gained popularity both on the web and in the offline world with the help of Trump and other elected officials. In Georgia, a candidate for Congress has hailed Q as a "mythical hero," and at least five other Congressional hopefuls from Illinois to Oregon have expressed their support.

One scholar found an increase of 71 percent in QAnon content on Twitter and an increase of 651 percent on Facebook since March.

Jon Thorngate is the pastor of LifeBridge, a non-denominational congregation of about 300 in a suburb of Milwaukee. His members have posted "Pandemic" on Facebook in recent months, he said, a half-hour film that portrays COVID-19 as a money-making scheme by government officials and others. Members also went around a now-banned Breitbart video, which promotes hydroxychloroquine as a virus remedy.

Thorngate, one of the few pastors who would go on record among those who found QAnon a real issue in their churches, said the videos are usually posted online by just five to 10 members. But he's found in discussions with other members that many more are prone to conspiracy theories than the ones commenting.

Thorngate partially attributes the phenomenon to the "death of expertise"—a mistrust of figures of authority that causes some Americans to undervalue long-established competency and knowledge steps. Among some members of the church, he said, the mentality is, "I will use the church for the things I like, disregard it for the things I don't like, and find my reality.

"That part is troubling for us because nothing now feels authoritative."

For years in the 1980s and 1990s, U.S. evangelicals, above almost any other group, cautioned of what would happen when people abandon absolute truth. (which they are found in the Bible), suggesting that the concept of partial reality will lead people to believe in something that reinforces their inner hunches. But big government skepticism, challenging scientific orthodoxy (on evolution, for instance) and denying Hollywood values and liberal elites took root among millennial Christians, many of whom felt politically marginalized and beaten up by mass media. For QAnon, they're normal targets.

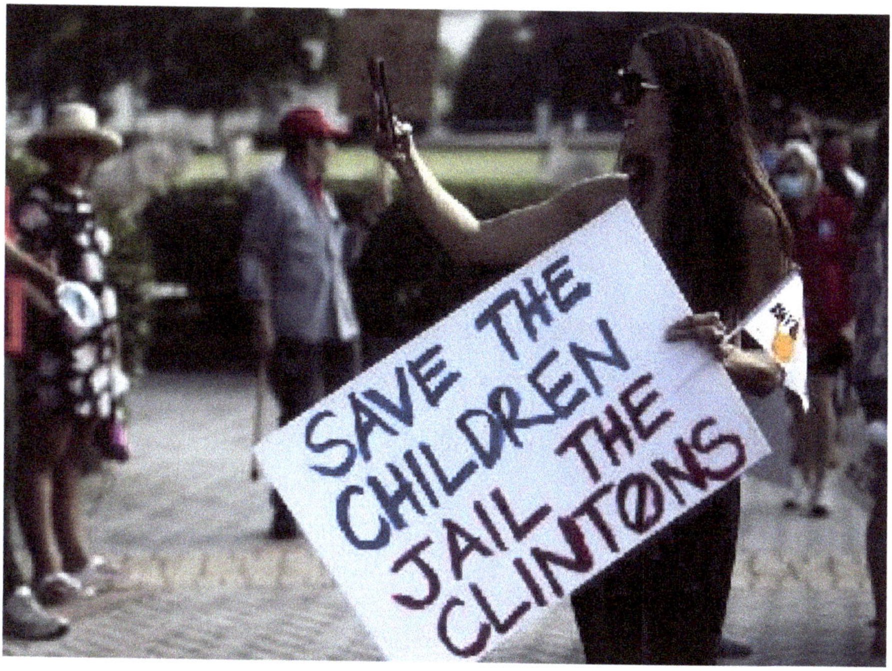
SAVE THE
CHILDREN
JAIL THE
CLINTONS

CONCLUSION

To be sure, QAnon remains a "popular-opinion fringe phenomenon," since research shows that "most people do not know what it is, let alone believe it," Dartmouth professor Nyhan said.

"But if their revealed philosophy encourages them to commit aggression, that is potentially dangerous," he said. "I am also concerned about the way believers in 'Q' have become more prominent and powerful online and inside the base of the Republican Party."

Earlier this month, a Republican primary runoff election in Georgia was won by far-right GOP congressional nominee Marjorie Taylor Greene, who has demonstrated support for QAnon theories. Trump had called her a "bright Republican Star" in a tweet.

The campaign also gained credence from Trump himself. When a reporter explained part of the movement's idea — that Trump himself is protecting the planet from a satanic cult of pedophiles and cannibals — the president responded: "Is that meant to be a bad thing? I'm willing to put myself out there if I can help save the planet from the problems I'm willing to do it."

Trump obviously "is more than happy to dabble in topics some people used to keep the lid on. "Happily, this isn't all that commonly believed. But being funny is disturbing because it is not something that's too far out of the norm.

Our hypothesis has resulted in a very large number of people getting some form of context for theories of conspiracy, but not everyone has fallen into action. We also know that theories of conspiracy are now being raised as an actual subject. We already know that many Americans have formed their own opinion and opinions on our government, but we're bringing up the issue of conspiracy theories because they're what drives and spreads the mistrust. They cause people to question their own beliefs and instead present a statement/theory/belief to people that provides some interpretation that is negative, not "educates." Theories of conspiracy are the small conflicts that exacerbate the bigger conflict. Although we don't actually think of them as dangerous or successful, they do play a part that turns our logic / commonsense over.

CPSIA information can be obtained
at www.ICGtesting.com
Printed in the USA
BVHW092308230221
600896BV00009B/1280

9 781954 320925